what's this guide about?

As a **young person in care**, you have the right to tell adults what your wishes and feelings are about how you are looked after. There are many things that need to be decided about what is happening in your life – like where you live, who you live with, who you see, what activities you do and what money you get. If you say what your wishes and feelings are, and the adults who look after you listen, then you are more likely to be happy.

This guide gives you tips on how you can have your turn to talk and take part in deciding how you are looked after. You will often hear this called 'having your say'. You can have your turn to talk in your **foster home**, in your **children's home**, at court, at **reviews** and other meetings, at school, at appointments with **health professionals** and at **family group conferences**.

This guide tells you what you need to know about having your say about how you are looked after. But things may be a bit different where you live, for example in Scotland other words may be used for the ways you are looked after. Your social worker, **key worker** or carer can help you if you do not understand.

? how can I use this guide?

1 Read this guide by yourself to find out how to have your turn to talk.

2 Read this guide with a friend and then talk with them about it.

3 Go through this guide with your social worker, **key worker** or carer – they can explain things that you don't understand.

4 There may be some words you don't understand in this guide. If you see a word in bold, **like this**, then you can find out what this word means on page 21.

If you find it hard to speak up, remember to talk as much as you can to the adults working with you – and use the tips in this guide.

what does 'having my say' mean?

There are some decisions that you can't make on your own. Like if you legally can see your parents. But, you social worker has to take into accoun your wishes and feelings when making decisions that affect you.

There are laws, like the Children Act, that say that all children and young people must be asked what their wishes and feelings are about things that affect their lives.

This means that the adults working with you – your carers and adults from **social services**, your school and health services – must find out and respect your wishes and feelings when deciding how to look after you (some adults call this 'finding out your views'). They must also find out the views of your parents and any other adults who look after you.

Many young people think that adults should make some of the really important decisions. But, you still have the right to talk through the reasons why a decision was made.

？ what age do I have to be to have my say?

Whatever your age, adults should ask you for your views. Many young people become more involved in making decisions as they get older.

？ does this mean I make the decision?

You have the right to say what your wishes and feelings are and adults must think carefully about what you say, but some things may be decided that you do not agree with.

You can choose if you want to take part in making big decisions such as how much you see your family, or smaller decisions like what activities you want to do.

how does my local authority decide how to care for me?

Your **local authority** uses the **care planning process** to make decisions about where you live, your contact with family, your education, your health, legal issues, money and other activities. There are four parts to the process: assessment, planning, intervention and **review**. Adults should ask you what your wishes and feelings are in every step.

1 Assessment is about finding out what you need. Your local authority has to find out what is going on in your life and decide what help or services you need. You and your family should be involved by saying what you think you need.

2 Planning is when you and the adults who care for you make a plan of action for how you will be looked after, both now and in the future. When making a plan, your social worker should ask you what you think will help you.

3 Intervention is when you are given the help you need. This might be extra support at school, family support, going to a doctor or doing activities. You should have your say in what services you think are best for you.

4 Review is when you and adults check that everything in your care is working for you. Your reviews are very important for you because that is when you have a chance to say what you are happy or unhappy with.

what are all these plans?

 **TOP TIP: You should always be given a copy of your care plan and other plans.**

You can have your say in all the plans about how you are looked after. Your care plan covers all areas of your life, but there are also plans for your health, education, where you live, contact with family and friends, your daily life and for when you leave care.

your care plan

By law, every looked after young person must have a care plan. It is made by you and all the other adults who are involved in looking after you. The care plan makes sure you are well looked after and says what has been decided about where you live, who you live with, your health, your education, religion, language and culture, and contact with your family and friends.

The care plan may change as things in your life change. At your **review** you should say if you feel any changes are needed.

your health plan and assessment

The health plan and assessment is to make sure that you are healthy and well. You may have to go and see a doctor or a nurse. You can talk through your health, ask about anything that you feel would make you healthier or talk about things that are worrying you. It is not just about medical things – you can talk about whether you are happy or sad, playing sports and sexual health.

your personal education plan

Every looked after young person must have a personal education plan. You will meet with the **designated teacher** at school to talk about what you need in your education. This is your chance to tell them what you are good at, what you need help with and any problems you have, like if you are being bullied.

You should meet with the designated teacher at least every six months – more often when you first enter care. If you feel your personal education plan is not helping you, or that it needs to be changed, then ask the designated teacher for another meeting.

your placement plan

A placement plan is about all the day-to-day arrangements about where you live, both now and in the future. When making this plan, you should say if you are happy or unhappy about where you live and if you want to change anything. Changes could be big things like moving to somewhere else, or small things like what clothes you need. Remember, adults should not move you to a new place without asking you what you feel about it.

your contact plan

The contact plan says how often you will see your parents, brothers, sisters and other relatives. Talking about this plan is often hard, and can be upsetting if you are not happy with what has been decided. Be clear about how often you want,

or don't want, to see people in your family. Ask the social worker to talk through what has been decided so you understand. Remember, decisions can change later on.

your pathway plan

The pathway plan sets out the support that you should receive to help you move towards living on your own. It will cover things like where you live, your health, your education, work, training, personal support, money and leisure. All looked after young people should have a pathway plan by their 16th birthday.

My teacher and I work out how things can be made better for me at school – it helps.

$8 \times 8 = 64$

$9 \times 8 = 72$

what is my review?

TOP TIP: The most important person at your review is you!

Reviews are meetings that the **local authority** must hold every six months for looked after young people. During the meeting, you and the adults who care for you will check that your care plan is working for you. If it is not, then it should be changed. It is important that you say what you want and think, so changes can be made. If you say what you want and think, then it is more likely that things will get better for you.

At the review, you and the adults who care for you check:

● that you are being looked after well

● that things that were decided before have been done for you

● if anything needs to be changed

● what plans need to be made for your future

● that you and your parents know about your care, and that you all have your say.

? where and when is my review?

Anywhere, anytime – it's your choice. It could be at your **foster home**, your **children's home**, at your **social services** office, at school or somewhere completely different like your youth club. The best place to have your **review** is where you feel most comfortable.

Having lots of people in reviews can make you nervous.

Your review should be after school and not on a day that you would usually go to a club or do an activity.

can I ask for a review?

Yes. If you feel something needs to be changed then ask your social worker or **independent reviewing officer** for a **review**.

who is the independent reviewing officer?

The **independent reviewing officer** (sometimes called the IRO) is the person who is in charge of your **reviews**. It is their job to check you are being well looked after. They must make sure that everyone knows your views. They should speak to you before and after a review to make sure they know what you want and that you understand everything.

You should tell the independent reviewing officer if there is anything that would make it easier for you to take part in the review and to speak up.

who will be there?

These people should be at your **review** meeting:

- you
- your social worker
- your foster carers or **key worker**
- **independent reviewing officer**
- sometimes your mum, dad or other relative.

Other people may also go:

- your **advocate**
- **foster carers' support worker**
- your **children's guardian**
- **health professionals**
- **independent visitor**
- leaving care worker
- your headteacher, head of year or **designated teacher**
- staff or managers from your **children's home**
- **youth offending team** worker.

If you want, or don't want, a specific person to be at your review, say so on your **consultation form** or tell your independent reviewing officer or social worker.

how can I have my say?

TOP TIP: You have a choice about how much you take part in making decisions about your care.

There are lots of things you can do to make having your say easier. Three ways to have your say are:

- you can tell adults your wishes and feelings (some adults call this **consultation**)

- you can write things down

- you can go to meetings and **reviews**.

telling adults your wishes and feelings

To have your say, you must be ready to speak up. Social workers, carers, **key workers**, teachers and other adults who look after you should ask you what your wishes and feelings are before a decision is made. You may have to ask adults to listen to and act on your wishes and feelings.

Talking to adults should be two-way: where they talk and listen to you, and you talk and listen to them. As things change in your life, keep talking to adults about how you feel.

My advocate talks for me and it really helps me get my point across.

Although it's sometimes scary to talk to people, it's worth it. Adults around you need to know what's best for you, but they might not get it right if you don't tell them how you feel.

One of the best ways to have your say is to talk to an adult who you feel comfortable with and who listens to you. Your social worker is probably the best person. If you trust your social worker then you can begin to talk through exactly how you feel. If they know what is going on in your life, it is easier for them to make things better for you.

but what should I say?

Talk about:

- how you feel and anything you are unhappy with, like how often you see your family

- what you think is best for you now, and what you want to happen in the future

- how you feel about speaking in meetings, and if you need someone to speak for you

- anything that you don't understand.

what if my social worker doesn't give me enough help?

If your social worker does not help you enough, you should find another adult that you can talk to. Another adult could be your foster carer, a teacher at school, your **key worker** or another adult you get on well with – like a youth worker. Some young people find it hard to talk to their social worker because they have lots of different social workers, the social workers are busy, or they do not trust their social workers.

If you still feel you need extra help, you can speak to your **independent reviewing officer** or an **advocate**. You can ask your **local authority** to put you in touch with an advocate. You can also contact a **children's rights service** if there is one in your area.

On page 19 of this guide there is a list of organisations that can help you.

TOP TIP: Make a list about what needs to be done, and cross things off once they have been done.

writing things down

Another way of having your say is to write down your wishes and feelings. Some young people write a list of everything they want to say before a meeting. If you write a list, you can use it at a meeting to help you to remember what you want to say. You can give the list to adults at the meeting to read if you are too nervous to speak. You can always ask an adult to help you write your list.

> In my last review I wrote down what I wanted and passed it to my carer for the review so that I didn't have to say it.

Play football
See my cousins
Help with my homework

? what is a consultation form?

You should be given a **consultation form** or be asked to fill out a form on a computer programme, like Viewpoint, before your **review**. The form might have a different name where you live, such as a **contributions form**, but it will have lots of space for you to fill in what your views are about how you are looked after.

You can use your consultation form to say:

● what you do and don't want to talk about at your review – like something you have done well, or problems at school or home

● when and where you want your review

● who you want and don't want to be there.

going to meetings and reviews

You should be invited to a lot of different meetings and appointments. Most young people have heard about the **review**, but there are other meetings where you can talk to adults and decide about your education, your health, your care plan, seeing your family or where you live.

? do I have to go to reviews and meetings?

You don't have to go to your **review** or other meetings, but it is best that you do. The review and other meetings are about you and your future. You should be there so that you can say what you want to happen.

You can choose whether to go to all of a meeting or only part of it. If you think you will get bored, tired or nervous, ask if you can have your turn to talk right at the start of the meeting – then you can leave if you need to. If you need a break at any point (you might be angry or upset), then you can ask to leave the room for a while.

? can anyone else come to a meeting with me?

Yes, you can take a friend or an **advocate** along to meetings with you. Having a friend or advocate with you can help you feel more confident about speaking out.

? what if I don't go?

Even if you don't go, you should talk to your social worker, carer or other adult before and after the meeting or **review**. Then you will know exactly what is happening, and you can tell them your wishes and feelings.

 **TOP TIP: If you go to your meetings and reviews, you will have more choice in what happens in your life.**

? what can I do to get ready for a meeting?

To get ready for a meeting or **review** you can:

- find out what the meeting is about – there should be no shocks or surprises

- ask the adult in charge of the meeting (sometimes called the **chair**) what will be talked about, and the best way to talk about it if it is difficult for you

- decide if you are going to the meeting or not

- think about things before the meeting so you know what you want to say

- talk to adults that you trust before the meeting and ask them to remind you about what you want to say

- write down what you want to say – you could give this to an adult in the meeting

- talk to the adult in charge of the meeting or review to let them know what you want to say

- ask somebody else to go with you if you are nervous

Hey M8 the best ting I can tell U is 2 talk 2 some1 bout things B4 U enter the room. Make sure U no wot U want 2 say

- tell an adult who is going to the meeting what you want to happen
- fill in the **consultation form**.

If you do these things then you will feel more confident and able to take part in making decisions about what will happen.

Express your feelings and opinions – and make sure that adults are listening to you.

? what do I have to do in the meeting or review?

You have to tell the adults in the meeting or **review** what your wishes and feelings are. The person in charge of the meeting should ask you for your views. If they do not, just say, 'Excuse me but…' or ask an adult to interrupt for you.

If you are asked a question, you don't have to answer it straight away. Ask for a little time to think about it. You can always get someone else to say what you think later.

You should never go to a meeting and have to decide about something then and there. You should always be given a chance to think about it beforehand. But if it does happen, you should ask for everything to be carefully explained to you.

? what if I'm nervous about saying something wrong?

Don't worry about being nervous or saying the wrong thing. Many young people are worried about saying the wrong thing, getting into trouble, or upsetting their parents or carers when they are all in a meeting together.

If you feel this way, then tell the **chair** or an adult you trust before the meeting begins. The chair or another adult can make sure that for part of the meeting your parents or carers are not there, so that you can speak honestly about how you feel.

It is very important that you do this. If you don't tell someone why you are unhappy, then it cannot be sorted out.

 **TOP TIP: After the meeting, talk through the decisions with your social worker and make sure you are happy.**

? what other help can I get?

You can get lots of different help to have your turn to talk. Make sure you tell your social worker or **independent reviewing officer** if there are any things that you might need.

● If you have a disability then you must be given whatever help you need to be able to have your say. For example, if you use a wheelchair, then the meeting must

Sometimes it's not the child that can't talk, it's adults that don't understand.

be held in a building that you can get into. If you need communication aids (such as computer packages or key working forms with signs and symbols), then they should be given to you.

● If you need an interpreter, one should be at the meeting.

● Any letters addressed to you should be written in the language of your choice.

● If you need help with reading, writing or understanding anything, this help should be given to you. You can also ask that the meeting be tape-recorded.

? what can I do after the meeting?

You should speak to the **chair** or your social worker after the meeting to make sure you know exactly what is going to happen. It is important that you understand what has been decided. Even if you don't like what has been agreed, you should be told why that decision has been made.

You should also be sent the **minutes** from the meeting. The minutes of the meeting should set out what was decided and who is going to do what. If you don't think the minutes say what happened at the meeting, you can write down what you think happened and send them back.

> Read the minutes and make sure you agree. And then chase up anything that is not done.

why do they always talk about things that aren't going well rather than things that are?

Adults will often talk about things that are not going well because they are trying to sort out any problems you are having in your care. But you should also have the opportunity to celebrate what you have done well. Tell your social worker or the person in charge of the meeting that you want to talk about the good things that you have done. Or just bring it up yourself!

how else can I take part in making decisions?

 TOP TIP: Now that you know how you can have your turn to talk, speak out and pester your social worker or carer to help you.

You should be involved in all the decisions that are made about how you are looked after, not just at your **review** but also when you meet with different people or get sent letters.

There are lots of ways to make it easier for you to have a say. If you think of something that would make it easier for you, then suggest it to your social worker or **independent reviewing officer**. For example, one young person had his **family group conference** held in a hotel.

Here are some other ideas.

- Ask to have your meeting in a relaxed place.
  The meeting could be in a place you feel comfortable, with sofas, pictures and toys, and where there are hot and cold drinks.

- Have one-to-one meetings with everyone who helps to look after you.
  Instead of having a review or meeting with everyone together in one room you could meet with just one person, like your social worker or independent reviewing officer, to discuss what you want and think about your care. For your review, the independent reviewing officer could meet everyone on their own, including you, rather than all at once, and then make a decision.

- Use a computer package or CD-ROM.
  There are computer packages, such as Viewpoint, that you can use to type in your views on a computer for your **local authority**. You can also use a CD-ROM, like SpeakEasy, where you and an adult

work out what you think is best for you. A lot of young people say computer packages are fun and easy to use – especially if they are too scared to speak in meetings.

● Use the phone or a tape recorder, make a video or write down your views on paper.
If you can't go or don't want to go to a meeting or review, your views could be given by phone or video link, a tape-recording or a letter you have written. An adult could help you do this.

● Have a meeting while eating a meal together.
You could have your review or other meeting while eating a meal together. This would make it more relaxed and enjoyable for everyone.

● Play a game or draw when you meet.
During the meeting or review, you could play games or do an activity like drawing to help you to talk about things.

It can be better to meet people individually, rather than everyone ganging up on you, because it does feel like that sometimes.

what if I'm unhappy?

TOP TIP: It is OK to complain. You won't get in any trouble, and things will change if you speak out.

If you're not happy about something – maybe your social worker never contacts you – you can complain.

You should try to sort out the problem by asking your social worker, carer or another adult to help you. If you are still unhappy you can make a formal complaint.

? how do I make a formal complaint?

There are lots of ways to do this.

1   You could ask the Independent Reviewing Officer at your meeting.

2   Your foster carer or keyworker can help you to make a complaint.

3   You can ask for an advocate or an adult who you trust to make a complaint on your behalf.

If I have a problem and I can't talk to my social worker about it, I go to the children's rights service.

who else can help me?

The organisations listed below can help you.
There are also some helpful websites, magazines and CD-ROMS.

UK-wide services

ChildLine
A free and confidential helpline
for any child in trouble or danger.
Helpline: 0800 1111
Website: www.childline.org.uk

Who Cares? Trust
Offers confidential advice to anyone
in care at present, or in the past.
Tel: 020 7251 3117
Email:
mailbox@thewhocarestrust.org.uk
Website:
www.thewhocarestrust.org.uk

Children's Legal Centre
Provides legal advice and
information services.
Tel: 01206 877 910
Email: clc@essex.ac.uk
Website:
www.childrenslegalcentre.com

services in England and Wales

National Youth Advocacy Service
Provides information, legal advice,
representation and advocacy.
Helpline: 0800 616 101
Tel: 01516 498 700
Email: info@nyas.net
Website: www.nyas.net

National Care Advisory Service
Runs projects for under-supported
young people.
Tel: 020 7336 4824
Email: nlcas@nlcas.org
Website: nlcas.org

Resolution
The association keeps a list
of Children's Panel Solicitors.
Tel: 01689 820272
Email: info@resolution.org.uk
Website: www.resolution.org.uk

services in England

Voice
Provides help to children in care.
Tel: 0808 800 5792
Email: info@voiceyp.org
Website: www.voiceyp.org

A National Voice
Run for and by young people
who are or have been in care.
Tel: 0161 237 5577
Email: info@anationalvoice.org
Website: www.anationalvoice.org

Children's Rights Director for England
The children's rights director's job is
to find out what young people and
children think about living away from
home or getting social services.
Freephone: 0800 528 0731
Email:
TheTeam.rights4me@ofsted.gov.uk
Website: www.rights4me.org

11 Million – Office of the Children's Commissioner for England
The Children's Commissioner works
with, and on behalf of, children and
young people to improve their lives.
Tel: 0844 800 913
Email: info.request@11million.org.uk
Website: www.11million.org.uk

services in Northern Ireland

VOYPIC (Voice of young people in care)
An independent regional voice
that seeks to empower and enable
children and young people with an
experience of care to participate fully
in decisions affecting their lives.
Tel: 02890 244 888
Email: info@voypic.org
Website: www.voypic.org

Northern Ireland Commissioner for Children and Young People

The commissioner's job is to promote the rights and best interests of children and young people.
Tel: 028 9031 1616
Email: info@niccy.org
Website: www.niccy.org

Children's Law Centre

Gives advice on children's rights and the law.
Tel: 028 9024 5704
Chalky freephone: 0808 808 5678
Email: info@childrenslawcentre.org
Website: www.childrenslawcentre.org

services in Scotland

Care Commission

Inspects and regulates care services.
Tel: 01382 207 100
Lo-call: 0845 60 30 890
Website: www.carecommission.com

Who Cares? (Scotland)

Acts as a voice of looked after young people.
Tel: 0141 226 4441
Email: enquiries@whocaresscotland.org
Website: www.whocaresscotland.org

Scottish Child Law Centre

Provides free legal advice.
Tel: 0131 667 6333
Freephone: 0800 328 8970
Email: enquiries@sclc.org.uk
Website: www.sclc.org.uk

services in Wales

Voices from Care

Run by people who have been in care to help young people who are or have been in care in Wales.
Tel: 029 2045 1431
Email: info@vfcc.org.uk
Website: www.vfcc.org.uk

Children's Commissioner for Wales

The Commissioner and his team are there to help make sure that children and young people in Wales know their rights, have a voice and get good services and opportunities.
Tel: 01792 765 600
Email: post@childcomwales.org.uk
Website: www.childcom.org.uk

Tros Gynnal

Operates advocacy schemes and an advice service for looked after young people.
Tel: 029 2039 6974
Freephone: 0800 581 862
Email: admin@trosgynnal.org.uk
Website: www.trosgynnal.org.uk

websites

www.carelaw.org.uk

This website covers many topics, from your rights in care to what happens when you leave care.

resources

My Life Story

Interactive CD-ROM for life story work with children and young people.
Tel: 01856 761 334
Website: www.information-plus.co.uk

SpeakEasy

Interactive CD-ROM that enables children and young people in care to express their wishes and feelings.
Tel: 01856 761 334
Website: www.information-plus.co.uk

The Who Cares? Magazine

A free magazine produced for and by young people in care.
Tel: 020 7251 3117
Email: mailbox@thewhocarestrust.org.uk
Website: www.thewhocarestrust.org.uk

Think Smart

A series of resources published by The Who Cares? Trust designed for children and young people in care:
● *Staying in School* – Interactive CD-ROM
● *Planning To Do Well* – Booklet
● *Bullying* – Cards
● *Moving Schools* – Wall Planner
Tel: 020 7251 3117
Email: sales@thewhocarestrust.org.uk
Website: www.thewhocarestrust.org.uk